I0822421

THE STAGGERING LOSS OF YOUR DOG

Some Ways to Get Through

Sarah Whitten-Grigsby

To All the Dogs We've Loved and Lost

Table of Contents

Introduction

The wording of the subtitle of this book has been chosen carefully. Far be it from me to say, 'How to get through the staggering loss of a dog,' because that would imply that I can make it easy for you, and the first thing I must tell you is that the only way through it is through it. We cannot go around it, under or over it. Anyone who says they can make this grief quick and less painful for you is either deluded or just plain dishonest. There is no easy way, no such thing as skirting this particular sorrow, but there are some sources of comfort which I hope will guide you through the deep grief of losing your beloved canine family member.

Herein are some revelations which will at least provide what I call 'cold comfort,' which means it's not much comfort but it's better than no comfort at all. That sounds discouraging but please don't give up hope.

As I write, my husband and I have four senior animals – three dogs and one cat – all in various stages of decline. I began this little book writing in real time about the loss of one of our dogs, and we have since lost him. Our senior Vizsla*, Basil ('Baz'), had a stroke about five months ago and when he seemed to have come back from it I drove him, with one of our rescues, Beasley, to Lemon Bay, which is a lovely preserve near us, for a walk. But Baz's back legs collapsed completely as soon as we got out of the van. So I picked him up – which is not easy with a tall, leggy, seventy pound dog – put him back in the van and drove us home. I call Baz my biological child because he was the only one of the current four who was not a rescue; we'd had him since puppyhood and got him from a breeder. Basil-rhymes-with-dazzle faded away from us as I wrote this little book, and as he did part of us faded with him, and so this writing is as timely and heartfelt as ever.

Read on, and may you find some salve for your gaping wound until enough time has passed that you can breathe again without weeping, and can live your Life After Dog in deepened compassion, in less woe and in immeasurable gratitude for having had the enormous gift of a dog.

I'll share my own dog stories with you and the ways in which I have learned to recover, albeit slowly, from the staggering loss of a dog.

*Vizslas are Hungarian Pointers

1

You're Not Crazy

My very first dog loss was in 2017. The nightmare began on an uncharacteristically dark, grey day in Florida. As we sat in the waiting room with several other people, each of us with our dog, anticipating the dreaded cancer diagnosis, a woman somewhere down the hallway lost her dog and began to keen and wail and shriek. This was our soundtrack as we awaited our turn.

The veterinary oncologist's exam room had charcoal grey walls and the oncologist herself was wearing grey. She had all the charm of an angry rhinoceros, which didn't help. Imagine having no bedside manner when your waiting room is full of people who are fairly certain their beloved dogs have cancer! The doctor jabbed her own finger while taking a blood sample from our dog, Wessex, had to leave the room to bandage herself, and then had to start again while my husband, Les, and I continued to hold our respective breaths. Then she pronounced Wessex cancerous.

On the drive home, under the bleak and threatening sky, I looked at Wessex dozing on the back seat and wished I could go with him. I thought I could not bear the loss of him, my first dog, my beloved child.

If you should die before me, ask if you could bring a friend.

- Stone Temple Pilots

That night, sleepless and haunted, I Googled, *Why is it harder to lose a dog than to lose a human loved one?* Now completely depressed and in full-fledged Nightmare Zone, I thought I was going crazy. Then I found a wonderful article online in Psychology Today* which helped me to understand my feelings and which I hope will help you.

First, the article said, for many, many people – not just you and me - it does indeed seem more painful to lose a dog than to lose a human. Why? Because dogs are our, "life witnesses," according to psychologist Julie Axelrod.** My own interpretation of this is that your dog has probably been with you as much as, if not more than, any human. If you have a spouse/partner, this may be true for you both. Or your dog may have been more attached to you than anyone else and thus spent more time with you. Either way, your dog has been as much as part of your daily life as breathing. Your dog has been a fully integrated family member – you wouldn't be reading this book otherwise – so almost every emotion and every life event you have experienced has been shared by your dog who has remained faithful, discreet and the best of companions.

There has been two-way empathy and a sort of symbiosis between you and your beloved dog, so of course you feel a different sort of sorrow and downright fear at the prospect of losing your dog. You are not crazy; you are losing a huge chapter of your life and thus a significant piece of yourself. The enormous amount of love you have shared is going away and, although it's right that your dog should take that with her or him, all of a sudden there will be nowhere for that love to go. That alone produces an empty, unanchored sort of near-desperation: a wretched sensation that the center of you is about to go missing. As Jamie Anderson, author of Doctor Who, said, "Grief is love with no place to go."

As our Basil declined, I often leaned into his velvet ears and whispered, "You will never know how much I love you."

One night toward the end he was running in his sleep. He was lying on his left side with his worst leg, the right rear, upward, and as his front legs twitched that back leg galloped and galloped. Years ago he and Wessex had run on the endless beach at St. Simon's Island when the tide was out. It was awe-inspiring to witness, and people on the beach pointed and smiled and gasped in delight as flocks of birds were sent into flight by the galloping dogs. Last night, as we watched him run and run in his sleep, Les said, "He's running on the beach at St. Simon's."

Baz! How well I remember holding you in the car as a new puppy, your eyes full of an older wisdom, after you'd chosen us. What will I do when you're gone? Life will continue, but part of me will always be waiting to join you on the other side.

*Psychology Today **Why Grief Over the Death of a Dog Is So Intense

Posted January 29, 2017
Frank T. McAndrew, Ph.D. *Out of the Ooze*

2

How Much Invasion to Inflict

Your dog is probably not worried about dying. As far as anyone knows, dogs don't worry about their mortality. Dogs differ from humans in this way, to the best of our knowledge. We worry obsessively about their short lives, but they don't. Their primal instincts sometimes kick in and if they are terminally ill they may isolate themselves, like wolves since time immemorial, so that the pack doesn't figure out that they are vulnerable. But, unlike us, your dog is probably not lying around thinking, "Oh, crap! I'm going to die!" This is cold comfort, but much better than worrying that your dog is not only ill, but also afraid or sad. As long as we don't pour our own sorrow onto them, they will carry on, letting their illness unfold or perhaps staying with us a bit longer.

If, on the other hand, we throw ourselves into our dog's warm furriness and sob – which I've done more times than I care to admit, as my nose runs onto their warm, velvet ears – the dog will probably sink faster. So, summon some false cheerfulness and try to hide it, at least from your dog, when the lump in your throat gets so big you can no longer contain your despair.

This is from my wise and deeply spiritual friend Suzan, who was losing her cat, Tommy, as we were losing Baz (Basil).

I have to slap myself when I catch myself feeling bad around Tommy. I ask WHY?????? They don't have the same problem going to Spirit that we do since they are so in touch with that (spirit) world. I saw Tommy leave his body and walk up to me twice one night while there he was, sleeping in the corner. I feel he is having a great time out of his weary body while he's sleeping. He misses our adventures, but he has a Spirit Buddy, Smokey, who passed in 2020 and is a Medicine Spirit. Smokey had a GREAT love for Tommy. I witnessed it when they met for the first time on the sidewalk about five months before Smokey took the Coyote Express to Spirit. Their meeting rivaled any meeting of dear friends. They teach us SO MUCH.

My husband says I'm a dog whisperer but the truth is I just listen, truly listen. How did you know he wanted that?! My husband asks in amazement. I just pay attention, I answer.

I often think about what a phenomenon it is that we can be so close to a non-human creature, develop this canine-human symbiosis and understand dog language so well, and yet we can't tell them what the Hell is happening when we have to put them under stress.

Take going to the vet, for example. Basil would start vibrating with anxiety as soon as we arrived in the veterinarian's parking lot and continue to shake in terror throughout the whole visit. It was bad for him and extremely stressful for me. No matter how small the chairs were – and he was a big fella -- he'd climb up behind me in the chair as though trying to hide. And I couldn't tell him that he was just there to be looked at and listened to and there might not even be a needle. (In fact, our most recent vet visit was for the purpose of getting him excused from the rabies vaccine officially, so he could still be licensed. I am of the mind that dogs are way over-vaccinated, but that's another book unto itself. Or at least an article. We do know that for some dogs – and definitely cats – the rabies vaccine can cause cancer. That's what a shelter vet told me.)

So there we were at the vet, Baz and me, and he was terrified and I was digging my fingernails into my palms and counting the minutes until we could get the hell out of there and go home to our sanctuary. How strange that despite all the communication flowing between us I couldn't put him at ease when he needed it the most.

And Heaven forbid you have to leave your dog at the vet! If you have a rescue dog and have to drop her or him off for some procedure, you cannot reassure him that he's not being abandoned again. This is why I never ask my rescue volunteers to take their fospice* dog back to the shelter vet for anything. I'd rather pay the extra money not to put them through the extreme stress. I'd rather sell a kidney, (one of mine, I mean), to pay the vet than have a shelter dog go back to the shelter for any reason. If I was an orphan who had finally been adopted and I had to keep going back to the orphanage on a regular basis I'd surely have a nervous breakdown, or at least poop on the exam table which is what Baz did once when he was at the vet and terrified.

So please keep all this in mind when your beloved dog is in decline. Don't rush her to the vet to be poked and prodded, tested and invaded, unless the situation is urgent, such as when a dog has respiratory distress. But if your dog is senior and slowly declining, just let her be a dog. When she can't be a dog anymore, then it's time to give the great gift of ending her suffering as painlessly as possible.

**Fospice Guardians are our foundation volunteers. Fospice means foster hospice and I prefer not to use 'owner,' when referring to animals. 'Guardian,' is a much more respectable description of the human caring for an animal. Our foundation name, ONE MORE DAY, comes from Joan Didion's book, The Year of Magical Thinking, in which she reveals that she and her family used to say to each other, "I love you more than one more day."*

3

Camouflaging Your Anticipatory Grief

It's inevitable that you will start to experience sorrow the moment you realize that your dog is in the last chapter of earthly life. This is called anticipatory grief.

While it's helpful to grieve right now so as to possibly ease the grief later, it's best to try not to let your dog know you're already anticipating her or his death.

If you can imagine being in your dog's paws – in decline and experiencing your loved one(s) moaning and weeping and waiting for your death -- it's an excellent indication that you should not let your dog know how sad you are. Hiding our sadness is difficult, but not impossible. In the last hours and minutes you will not be able to, nor should you try. By then, your dog will most likely be eager to pass from pain to peace and will be comforted by your presence no matter what your affect.

But in the weeks leading up to those final moments, if we constantly inflict our sorrow on our dogs, they will probably give up sooner. So, try to let your dog's decline happen as organically as possible, without adding to it. And try to remain cheery around your revered, canine, family member. It may also uplift your own spirits not to stay focused on the end, but rather to try and stay in the moment while there is still life coursing through your dog's veins. This simply means not using a funereal tone of voice or exuding an attitude of hopelessness when you're with your dog.

I've recently been reminded of this – see Suzan's comment below -- because Baz, at almost fourteen years old, had a five month decline. He seemed to be having small strokes after which he clearly showed signs of dementia. Then he would come back to us. The day of his first stroke we found him on the floor, sort of oddly crouched and confused. His long, slender back legs were barely working but he got himself up and away from us and as far out in the front yard as he could go, as though we were suddenly the enemy. I finally went weeping outside with this leash to bring him in and continued to weep intermittently for hours while checking on him, and at the same time trying to keep my distance. When I told Suzan this, she said the following extremely helpful things:

I hope you add the essential of keeping a joyful heart. No one can say when a being leaves our sight and embrace, and we rob them of our love and diminish their energy by inviting the specter of loss while they are still with us. We miss all the treasures.

And they feel we have given up on them and given up on their possibility of thriving even in small ways. We close our hearts to the miracle of life, with our limited sight, by donning the shroud of grief! Meanwhile, the dog is like: "HEY! I'm still here! I'll let you know what I need if you listen and we can still share our joy of my life. And then when I go to Spirit, adjust your sight and you will feel me with you in so many ways. Love is forever!

4

Bucket List Days

Let's face it, if you love your dog so much you feel that part of you is dying as your dog is dying, you have probably given that dog a wonderful life. The problem is, those of us who are highly responsible caregivers always feel as though we could have or should have done more.

Regrets can kill us, so if your dog is declining for the last time and there is something you wish you had done, for Heaven's sake, do it! I don't mean you have to travel to some faraway land and climb a steep mountain with the dog on your back, but just make sure you are loving that dog, feeding him his favorite treats or massaging his arthritic hips and legs, making sure he is sleeping on the cushiest possible surface, giving him peace and quiet while not leaving him alone too long, etcetera. Make the last chapter a beautiful one. Then you don't have to second guess yourself later.

Even as I write, one of our ONE MORE DAY Foundation Fospice Guardians, Amber, is giving her fospice dog a bucket list weekend. She's had the Pit mix, Shelbe, for about twenty months and loves her dearly. Shelbe came to us through a shelter and already had kidney disease, and last week she was diagnosed with a brain tumor and her back legs have been giving out. We have set up euthanasia for a few days hence and in the meantime Shelbe is having an ultra-special weekend, complete with car rides, which she loves, hot dogs, a trip to the beach and lots of love from all those who have gotten to know her during the time Amber has had her. I haven't met Shelbe, but I'll grieve for her. Our little foundation will pay for her in-home euthanasia, private cremation and return of ashes. Not all of our Fospice Guardians want or need this, but for those who do, we make every effort to provide it.

Whether or not you have the resources, time and energy to give your dog a bucket-list experience, please put in perspective all the good you have done for and with your dog. Focus on the positive, acknowledge that any negatives are minor, and let them go. The good times far outweigh the bad for those of us who truly love and care for our dogs.

Let go of your despair. Keep only the golden memories, which will be countless.

5

The Two Dilemmas

Invariably, it seems, our dogs have crises on the weekends or in the wee hours, when no vet is open and two options remain:

1) rush the dog to the veterinary Emergency Room, or
2) allow the dog to suffer until our vet's office opens.

There is no easy answer to this. Recently, a woman we know sat up all night with her actively dying dog, even when pain set in, rather than rush her to the ER which is unreasonably expensive, not to mention terribly stressful for the dog and for you, and not a peaceful way to go. I was in favor of her not rushing the dog to the ER, but I don't know how much pain the dog was in. She did get a painkiller into her dog, which visibly helped eased some of the suffering. And this was a dog who chose to be alone with her suffering, and tended to isolate herself from the family when she wasn't feeling well. There is no easy answer to this off-hours dilemma, except to follow your instincts.

We never want to prolong suffering, but nor do we want to add to the suffering with a bumpy car ride and a rush into the unfamiliarity of an emergency clinic. Sometimes you can wait another day or through a night, and sometimes you just can't. If there's respiratory distress or any other terrible struggle, then best to suck up the expense, if you can, and get your dog to the animal emergency clinic for euthanasia as quickly as possible.

The other dilemma occurs when you have scheduled euthanasia and then your dog has a significant resurgence. As I write, this is just happening to friends whose Jack Russell is in end-stage kidney disease. Their trusted vet was clear that it was time to let go, so they scheduled euthanasia and then their adored dog suddenly felt better, started eating again and showed some renewed energy. Their quandary was one of second guessing themselves. Having been told that their beloved dog's numbers were beyond Stage 4 kidney disease and there is no Stage 5, they decided to stay with the plan. When she was euthanized she had obviously been feeling better, but she didn't die in pain and suffering which she otherwise probably would have. They are still unsure if they did the right thing, but I believe that they did.

This resurgence often happens once a dog seems to have hit rock bottom. No one knows why, but so many dogs seem to have a very good last couple of days. However, if you have made the decision to let your sweet dog go, the vet has been clear, and your dog has, up to the last day or so, been obviously suffering, try not to second-guess yourself. If you postpone the euthanasia, as sure as God made little green apples your dog will sink again, badly, and during some hours when the only option, once again, is to rush her or him to the veterinary emergency clinic.

Once you have made the decision, you should probably stay with it.

6

Euthanasia

In 2016 I created ONE MORE DAY Foundation to give back to dogs for all they give to us. We are a network of volunteers placing homeless hospice dogs in loving, forever homes and helping to sponsor the veterinary costs to keep them comfortable throughout last breath. When I gave weekly webcasts the one most well-attended was about euthanasia.

Euthanasia is the big question, the ever-painful decision and the final gift we can give to a dog who is suffering. Are we playing God when we make the decision to send a dog, "over the rainbow bridge?" I don't know. I believe we are using our human powers to ease the passage from this life to the next; to be compassionate shepherds for this four-legged soul who has immeasurably enriched our lives. And some of us wish this for ourselves when the time comes! That is, we don't want to be kept alive to suffer and live a miserable quality of life for the sake of those who love us.

I have had only one animal, a beloved, sweet cat named Harley die naturally, and in retrospect I wish I had had him euthanized. He was my first animal, suffered for a week, and I didn't know any better. I thought I should leave him alone and not interfere with the death process and I also couldn't face the prospect of having him put down on a cold, metal table. I probably didn't even know about in-home euthanasia then, and certainly couldn't afford it. To let him slowly die was probably not the right decision. Now I know better.

If performed properly, euthanasia should be peaceful and virtually painless. It should consist of two injections: the first to literally put the dog to sleep and the second to stop the dog's brain, which in turn stops the heart. The process wasn't always as humane and can still be disturbing if the veterinarian isn't skilled or something else has come into play, such as an insufficient amount of the chemicals for the weight of the dog.

We've had an in-home euthanasia by a veterinarian who was highly skilled but talked too much. I found this inappropriate and disturbing, as we had otherwise created a very peaceful, quiet setting. Beware of vets who are all about ego which, mercifully, not all of them are. In all fairness, that too-talkative vet was probably trying to ease his own way through the deeply emotional experience of putting down our beloved dog, but still. I've read that vets are so busy studying other stuff they don't take classes in how to handle the emotional aspect of a euthanasia.

When do we make the decision for euthanasia? There are various lists you can find online which enumerate what to watch for, such as your dog's loss of interest in food and inability to get outside without assistance. But the main thing is to listen and watch for your dog's signals that enough suffering is enough and it's time to go, and then to stay with it throughout your dog's last breath.

It has been written – by a vet who chose to remain anonymous – that all dogs want in these last moments is the familiarity of our presence. Dogs want the sight of us if they can still see, the smell of us and, if they can still hear, the sound of our soothing voice. Without that, they can experience terror and confusion and thus an unpleasant passage.

I don't believe we die alone, if we have even one hand on us as we transition, and that's what shepherding is. I like to think of shepherding as gently handing off your loved one – dog or person – into the loving, 'arms,' of whatever is awaiting us beyond the harsh shackles of this life. If we do this, there should be no moment of fear and aloneness for the dying one during the process.

But some people go to appalling lengths to avoid having to make the decision for euthanasia for a dog, let alone stay with the dog throughout last breath. This is why so many senior, ailing dogs are "surrendered," to shelters. The truth is they are abandoned at the shelters, so that someone else will make the decision, hand it off to the shelter and also let the shelter pay for it, monetarily. I know this because the Executive Director of our local shelter told me so in detail. Often the owner has died and the dog is not wanted by the family or is found wandering, but other times the owner does not want the responsibility or expense of end-of-life care for a dog.

On our street a beautiful, senior German Shepherd was abandoned because, said the owner,

"She's been a great dog for fifteen years and she was great with the kids when they were little, but now we think she'll just go into the woods and die."

So saying, they shut her out of the house. The queenly dog, emaciated and arthritic, wandered our street where she lived, and was subsequently rescued by a divine woman who became one of our Fospice Guardians. She called the dog Shellbelle – she had been, "Shelly," -- and gave her ten weeks of loving care and adoration until Shellbelle became unable to walk and was clearly suffering. Then she was euthanized at the Fospice Guardian's home with a small group of us around her. It was a completely peaceful and deeply loving transition. Shellbelle was a magnificent dog and taught us grace. She exemplified gentleness and dignity despite the extreme hardship she endured after being shut out of her home.

Staying with our dog during euthanasia is agonizing and almost unbearably sad, but we must see it through if we are to have no regrets. I knew a woman who dropped her beloved dog off at the vet for euthanasia, and then drove away, and she has been haunted by that decision for all the years since. My friend and dog rescue partner, Silvia, has been asked, more than once, to take someone's dog to be euthanized because the someone couldn't face doing it. But, barring any extreme circumstances in which we absolutely are unable to be with our dog, we have to face it. It's our responsibility. If given the chance, our dogs will stay with us throughout our last breath, and we owe them the same. So, whether at home or at the vet's, please, stay with your dog!

Preparing for euthanasia can include loving rituals. There is much to be said for setting up a lovely atmosphere during your dog's transition. If you're at home it can be peace and quiet, or soft music or some sounds of nature, candles, and anything that will make your dog feel relaxed and safe and make you feel not so powerless. And you can certainly take some soft music or nature sound effects with you to the private space at the vet's if you are having euthanasia there. (Not candles, of course, unless they are battery powered.) Take what supports you and stay with your dog afterward if you need and want to. My friend Jane uses in-vet's euthanasia and she stays with her dog for an hour or more afterward, just sitting and reflecting, talking quietly to her dog and grieving.

When Basil's back legs gave out for good we quickly called for in-home euthanasia. The vet we have used in the past was unavailable, but our good friend, Silvia, who is a nurse and who is now certified to perform euthanasia for dogs, was able to come on short notice the next day.

We gave Baz two strong dog tranquilizers and two very effective calming chews, and he lay beside our bed, which was the last place he had collapsed. We got towels underneath him because when euthanasia is performed there is often a sudden outpouring of various bodily fluids.

Baz was very pleasantly stoned, as far as we could tell, when Silvia arrived, and he never even flinched at the IV. Our beloved child went quickly to sleep as I whispered sweet nothings in his ear and my husband, Les, sat nearby. At some point I noticed that our other two dogs had come silently into the room and each lay down on the rug. This can be a good thing, because then it seems that the other dogs understand and do not spend the ensuing weeks and months looking for their step-sibling, who is not coming back.

During the second and final injection, as Baz slept heavily, I continued to tell him how much we would love him forever, asked him to give our love to Wessex and told him we'd see them on the other side*. And then he was peacefully gone. I moved away then, not wanting to feel him without his heart beating.

We carried him out to the van where I'd prepared a bed of blankets, and drove him to the funeral home for individual cremation. I did put my hand on him there, and only felt his familiar, soft warmth. I fell apart completely then and everyone was very kind and empathetic. I was later told that the funeral home staff didn't even want to ask me to sign paperwork and had Les sign it when he went back, calmly, four days later, to pick up Basil's cremains.

Baz is with us in an oak box in our bedroom now, beside Wessex and Lily, and we can talk to him when we pass by. When I lay hands on the box I can almost hear him galloping along the beach, long ears flying, and I am reminded that he had a wonderful life.

* I believe this: that we will all be reunited in that next exquisite dimension. We may not be able to imagine what it will be like, nor have the words for it, but I believe we will be united with our loved ones for all eternity.

7

You Are Not Alone

Back to Wessex, who gave me my first experience with losing a dog. We had Wessex for nine weeks after his lymphoma diagnosis. Nine, agonizing weeks during which I was repeatedly told that he would let us know when the time came. And so he did. One day his legs gave out and we called and set up an appointment for in-home euthanasia a couple of days later. The next day he had a resurgence and came for his daily walk, so we postponed the appointment. But that night he walked toward me as I sat on the floor and when I reached out and touched him he cried out in a way I had never heard before, and that was his way of saying he'd had enough. In the morning he stood in front of the shower looking at me as if to say, See what a good boy I am? So I gave him a quiet, gentle, warm shower, and then we gave him a heavy-duty veterinary tranquilizer, and he lay on the rug in the living room sun with us. I put candles in his dog bowl on the rug in front of him, and found low-key surf sounds on the Alexa and he stared, in a trance, at the flickering flames and never even flinched when the first injection went into his thigh. We told him how much we loved him and what a good boy he was and I whispered that I'd see him on the other side. And then the second needle went in and he was gone. My husband still had hands on Wessex then, but I didn't touch him after he was gone because, as with Baz six years later, I needed to remember the feel of him with his life force still flowing.

I went out to the back yard and wailed and keened and thought I would die of grief. But the next day I actually experienced a tiny bit of short-lived relief, knowing that the worst was over and he was no longer suffering and we could get on with the business of recovering. I had already been grieving for nine weeks, and there is much to be said for grieving in the moment. There will be a bit less suffering later if we grieve right now.

When I am losing a dog, I take comfort in the realization that millions of us have been through this and truly understand how it feels. We are/you are not alone. Whereas there will always be private, individual, unique aspects of our grief, many of the feelings of losing a dog will have been and are being experienced right now by millions of other humans, even as you and I are experiencing them.

Those of us who feel the enormity of the loss are not the ones who have, "a pet," we kept on the periphery of our lives and looked upon as something that had to be walked twice a day and was otherwise on the margins of our lives and sometimes an inconvenience. We are not the woman who got a dog from our local shelter and then returned him because he was shedding in her house. And we are not the people who decide, when our dog is old and ill that we'll, "surrender it," to the shelter so someone else can deal with the expense or so someone else can make the decision for euthanasia.

Instead, we are the people who have loved our dogs, cats and other animals as much as is humanly possible. They are, after all, our children. There's no need to compare them to human children, nor ever to say that losing a dog is as hard as losing a child. Nothing can be harder than losing one's human child, and that's not the point. The point is that our animals rely on us for everything: for food and shelter and safety and kindness and lots of exercise. Without us, dogs cannot survive, and so they are, indeed, our children.

We love and respect our dogs. So when this dear creature who is truly a family member begins to decline and the end is at hand, the enormous sadness we feel has been and is being experienced by a dogillion other humans. I find this helpful to know, partly because it's so easy to focus, instead, on all the people who are astoundingly cruel and thoughtless where their animals are concerned. We are not. I'm with you. I get it. When you're up in the night grieving, by virtue of our similar losses, millions of us are with you in spirit. I stand with you, and you are standing with me.

8

Remains

For some of us, it's a great comfort to keep our dog's remains as ashes returned after private cremation or, where legal, to bury our dogs on our property. For others, there is no desire to have the remains as it may be a painful reminder. If you choose not to have remains returned you can leave the remains at the vet for mass cremation, which means several dogs will be cremated together and remains not returned to you. Sometimes I think this is fine because it means none of the dogs – albeit their physical remains only -- are alone during that process.

If you live in a state like Florida where it's legal to bury your dog in your yard, you can choose to take the dog home after euthanasia, or, in the case of in-home euthanasia, keep the body for burial. Otherwise, most in-home vets will take the remains with them, either for private or mass cremation. It usually takes about a week for return of ashes. Some pet crematories provide a little plaque with the dog's name on the box/urn, but I prefer to receive the ashes back in their carved, wood box with no plaque and to create and word my own plaque. This is very easy and inexpensive to do online; Amazon sells a variety of custom plaques.

If your dog has passed away naturally, you may either have to drive the body to a pet crematory or have the body picked up by a service which does the transport to a crematory. The latter can be expensive, however.

Remember, this is just the outer shell; once a dear, dog body that ran and played, but now just a crippled shadow of that healthy, young being. Your dog's spirit now flies, unburdened, and will be with you always.

9

Deep Grief

By the time you have lost a loved one, be it dog or human, you are on your way to becoming well-versed in the art of grieving. For all that has been written about grief and the stages of it, I believe I have realized something new: that a significant part of grieving is dread. Ten months after we lost our mother, my siblings and I lost a sister very suddenly. In comparing notes we agreed that we were experiencing dread, as we faced our second round of deep grief so soon after the first.

With grief we dread the pain we will feel, we dread life without the loved one and how we will face daily life with this significant part of us missing and while trying to carry on despite the agonizing emptiness.

In the case of losing a dog, there can also be a strange sensation of loving your dog so much that she or he can never really know and can never return the undying love. It's a kind of emptiness that results from dogs not being able to understand everything we say and from us not being able to convey everything to them. We can convey so much to our beloved dogs, but not these fine points: *I'll be back. I'm not leaving you.*

This will only hurt for a few seconds. This will make you feel better. We'll go home soon. I love you more than life itself. Thank you for being such a wonderful dog. Yes, of course they feel loved – whatever that feels like for a dog -- but that's different from being able to understand the fine points.

But back to deep grief. Time heals much, if not all, of this. There comes a time when we can look back and feel more gratitude than sorrow, believe me. We will always love and miss this dog, but as we begin to surface we will truly appreciate the magnificent times we had together. Remember; nothing can ever take away what you and your dog have shared. It is as much a part of you as breathing.

In the meantime, having said all that about not being alone in this experience of losing a dog, I must also tell you that in my experience some moments of grief will be, must be, solo, and this is what will move you along and eventually lift you up and out of the darkness. Because when we are in the deepest grief, the distraction of other people is not always helpful. The pain is there every waking moment anyway. (And possibly in our sleep, too.) That initial grieving, the first few days and weeks and months - but hopefully not years – has to be helped along by some moments of solitude and has to unfold when you are alone, or only with those who share in your deep grief and have also lived with and loved this dog. No amount of support or love or advice can really ease our initial sadness and shock. If you have not allowed yourself to experience your grief in quiet solitude, to shriek and wail and holler at the Heavens, you will have tamped down your grief and it will last longer. At least this is my firm belief, based on extensive experience. Better that you have a day of solo agony to assist in the process of healing than go out with a group of jolly friends and try to pretend that nothing is wrong. This doesn't mean you have to isolate yourself from your family or those who are also in deep grief, but it means putting your head down and slogging through the messy, weighty, extremely painful sorrow in some moments alone.

During this time, don't let anyone tell you that you need to get over it, snap out of it or just go get another dog. Anyone who makes a flippant comment, albeit perhaps with good intentions, has absolutely no idea what you are going through. That person has not loved and lost a dog. Anyone who marginalizes the loss of your four-legged child does not understand, at all, what you are experiencing. But I do. And so do more people than we can count.

10

Self-Protection

During deep grief, immediately after loss, we are extremely vulnerable. We become thin glass or fine crystal and feel as though if someone so much as looks at us we'll shatter into a dogillion pieces.

When my sister, Annie, died suddenly, I was afraid to leave the house, even to go to the grocery store. I felt as though one of my limbs had been ripped off and I was bleeding profusely, but no one would be able to see it. Someone might come up to me and say innocently, "Would you like to try a sample of the new and improved Tofurkey?" And I would crack into shards and then implode, causing a scene.

If you absolutely have to be out and about, at work, for example, try to protect yourself. You can actually tell people, "My dog has just died and I can't breathe right now." Do this in person or via email or text. Tell your boss or, if you're the boss, tell your employees. There is always risk attached to telling people something extremely sensitive, but the protection it will probably afford you in this case should outweigh anything insensitive someone might say, hopefully.

You can always just not respond when someone says something unintentionally insensitive or waits for you to smile or even laugh over a clever remark. If we just stare, nonplussed, people are bound to get the hint and leave us alone. Silence often is, as the saying goes, the most powerful response.

The problem with confiding in people that you've just lost your dog is that it does render you vulnerable. When Wessex died, only one person made a callous, thoughtless remark, and I didn't get upset because I already knew this woman to be completely lacking tender sensibilities. There I was, deep in anticipatory grief and when I mentioned that Wessex had cancer she announced harshly – in between long drags on her filterless cigarette – "You'll get another dog!"

But everyone else was thoughtful and gentle, understanding and deeply respectful. I probably got as many condolence cards as I received when my dear mother died. And oh, how I appreciated that. Thank you.

Now Basil is gone, too – just a week as I write this part – and I decided to post this on Facebook. The people who surfaced who knew him in New York when he was young and here in Florida at the dog beach for many years, wrote beautiful tributes and understand what a sweet gentleman and lovely companion he was. I had first felt the need to be private about the loss of him and not post, and was then so glad I had posted! There was sadness far and wide at the loss of Baz, and I have acknowledged that the loss is not just ours. This situation may be true for you, too; that other people knew and loved your dog and will need to express their sadness to you. And listening to that will help you to grieve and to begin to heal. Once again, we are not alone.

11

Memorializing Your Dog

The long and short of it is, you will know exactly what you want to do to memorialize your beloved dog. You may feel the need to have a service. You might have a little shrine outdoors; whether your dog was cremated or buried in the back yard. You might have the ashes inside on your mantel or in your bedroom, like me. You might just have photos or some sort of marker, or maybe none of the above, and instead just commit everything to memory. Many rescues and shelters also offer acknowledgement with a memorial donation in your dog's name. You can donate or let others who wish to contribute donate to the local shelter in your dog's name.

There are pet grave markers and anything else you could possibly imagine, pretty much, available online, many not expensive.

Over our bed I have a framed collage of enlargements of Wessex running on the beach and swimming in the ocean water at the Outer Banks in North Carolina. Looking at them I am reminded that he had a wonderful life.

While he was declining, I made a ten-minute video of his life and it helped me along, although now, almost six years later, I can't watch it. I don't know who can; not even my sister, who knew him. But he is very much with us, in countless excellent memories, photographs, stories and in spirit. Wessex lived a full life, but it wasn't long enough, of course. The average length of a Vizsla life is twelve years and he only lived to eleven. Basil outlived him by almost three years, and that's still not long enough. I'll be creating some sort of photo and video tribute to Baz in due course.

My stepson just told us the story of a man who raises Great Danes on human food and they are living – instead of about nine years – to be seventeen, eighteen and nineteen. This is amazing for a large breed dog. How we all wish dogs lived so much longer than they do!

Our fighty-bitey rescue Rat Terrier, Lily, lived to be seventeen as small breed dogs often do. But the bigger the dog the shorter the life and that seems grossly unfair.

My husband and I are both quite tall, and I've often wondered if our lives will be shorter because of it! But by now we're well into our senior years, so I guess being large breed won't be what takes us.

12

What About Cats?

I know: this is a book about dogs. But I love cats, too, and have had some extra-special ones. Crabby Kitty made quite the splash and had a small Facebook following as well as fans among those humans who met him in person. He had been adopted from our local shelter and returned to the shelter some years later, old and deaf. The shelter called me to ask if I could place him and I brought him home instead. He came to us as Conor.

The shelter vet gave Conor a couple of weeks to live, and we had him for two years, during which he was adored. Because he used to shriek in the night*, and sounded furious, I began to call him Crabby Kitty, and everyone took to that name.

He was grey and handsome in a senior kind of way and incredibly sweet, for a cat who had been passed around for God knows how many years or how many times.

One day, Crabby fell ill and I knew he was nearing the end. He was sick from both ends and so once he quieted down I took him into the shower with me because he liked water. I held him like a baby, gently washed all the sickness off him and then swaddled him in a towel, and he was revived and lasted another couple of months. When the time came to let him go we had a local veterinarian come to the house.

Crabby sat on my lap and didn't react at all while the vet gave him the first injection. After a minute or two, he went into a sort of trance, staring into the distance. Then she gave him the second and he quietly passed from this life to the next, still in my lap. We buried him in the back yard under a Norfolk Pine tree with a sleeping angel garden statue. I loved him dearly.

We now have another cat who was supposed to be hospice. She had cancer at the shelter and a life expectancy of a year. We've had her for four and a half years so far.

My point is not that shelter vets are always wrong, but that loving care can bring a dying creature back to life. But you already knew that.

*Night shrieking from a cat can apparently sometimes be a symptom of a thyroid problem. Crabby was deaf, and so I thought maybe that was why he shrieked. In any event, it was a frightening sound, as though someone was being murdered.

13

Surfacing

You'll know when and if you will want to get another dog. Nothing can replace the dog you've lost, but another divine four-legged soul can certainly soothe the wound and eventually fill the empty space. And who knows? Sometimes just when you said you'd never get another dog – because you can never go through the loss again – you reluctantly take another dog into your life and that dog becomes the dog of your heart. Or another dog of your heart; an enormously comforting, loving, hilarious, playful, warm, soft canine gift you can't believe you've found, and you are so grateful that you took the chance.

If you're senior, please don't get a puppy. If you pre-decease a young dog he or she will probably wind up in a shelter, since often families don't want a dog they stand to inherit. At ONE MORE DAY we encounter these situations all the time. Only those of us in dog rescue know how we scramble and scrounge to help as many dogs as we can, when someone has died (of all the nerve!) and left the dog with no Plan B. People not looking at the big picture never cease to amaze me. Sometimes an ill or rickety human becomes unable to take care of the dog or goes into a nursing home and whoever doesn't want to take the dog opens a door and lets the dog wander away, lost and confused, to try to live on the streets. This is highly irresponsible, not to mention cruel.

When one of these stray, elderly dogs is picked up and brought to a shelter, if in ill health and neglected condition – considered hospice -- we are asked if we can find a home. We often do, but we are a very small rescue, sustained entirely by private donations, and can't afford to sponsor as many dogs as we wish.

Almost all our hospice dogs are senior, and senior dogs are usually lovely and quite low maintenance. They don't need as much exercise or attention as young dogs and they make perfect companions for senior humans and other senior dogs. Senior dogs sleep a lot and mostly want comfy places to lie, good food, and maybe one slow walk a day.

But countless dogs of all ages need loving homes, so wait until you have emerged from deep grief before you make a firm commitment not to get another dog. In some cases it's the right thing not to get another, and in many cases getting another dog is the best thing you can do for yourself, for the dog, and for the world.

14

In Summary: The Hardest Moments

These are better summarized after the fact, if possible, so you don't have a list of things to dread right up front! There are five especially agonizing times during the death of our dogs:

1) When you first see the decline that will lead to euthanasia or natural passage. This is where anticipatory grief begins. Try to enjoy the good moments that remain.

2) Awaiting the vet for euthanasia, whether at home or in the animal hospital. If you are at home waiting and the vet runs significantly late, this can be torture. Try to set a lovely scene for your dog – with tranquilizing things such as veterinary Xanax or CBD dog calming chews or both, peace and quiet or some soothing sound effects, a soft place to be, or whatever special treat or special dinner your dog has liked during the good days. Keep yourself occupied in this way and talk to your dog, saying whatever you feel needs to be said before this Bon Voyage. That part is for you.

3) During euthanasia as you watch the life of your dog slip away. Focus on whispering into his or her ear, as the belief is that they can still hear us after the first injection. Lay hands on and feel your dog's warmth. Take deep breaths.

4) The minutes, hours and days immediately after your divine, beloved dog has left this earthly life. Don't be afraid to shriek and wail. I mean it. Do whatever you need to do to express and eventually release the enormity of the loss.

5) Even if it's been your conscious choice, the fifth shock is receiving our dog's ashes back in an urn. It's a stab in the heart, but ultimately a great comfort for some of us. I often lay hands on the urn – a carved, wood box – of Basil's ashes and talk to him, and it brings me comfort. I also feel comforted to know where his former, physical body is. I can still imagine the gently* doggish smell of him when I used to lean my forehead against his, bridge of nose to bridge of snout, so we were almost interlocked. (*Vizslas are known for not being stinky.)

15

Afterword

How I hope you have discovered something helpful and supportive in this book! Each dog loss experience differs from any other, and each presents its own challenges and sorrows. But the rewards for loving a dog far outweigh the agony of the loss. The light each dog soul brings into the world is a privilege and honor to experience, just as we willingly and gladly share our own light with these divine creatures. I am convinced that the human/animal bond is a sacred one and those of us who have a bond with animals are greatly enlightened. Those who have not are missing out on one of this earthly life's greatest gifts. And those who are cruel to animals, may they learn before it's too late. And if they don't, well, I believe they will answer for it one way or another, here or in the hereafter.

It's ironic how loving animals are to us, despite the fact that the human race has been so cruel to animals so much of the time. Now we can honor our beloved animals in whatever way we wish, and I believe that somewhere, on some level, they know that we honor them with every fiber of our being.

We do learn from our dogs, and they learn from us. This is as it is meant to be.

I wish you a dog-filled life, (or cat-filled, or horse-filled, etc.), and all the joy that comes from respecting and caring for a non-human sentient being. May your beloved dog's spirit fly high!

Godspeed!

www.ingramcontent.com/pod-product-compliance
Lightning Source LLC
Chambersburg PA
CBHW031956040826
48979CB00041B/43

* 9 7 8 1 9 6 2 1 0 2 5 3 7 *